F FOR EFFORT!

More of the Very Best Totally Wrong Test Answers

Richard Benson

CHRONICLE BOOKS
SAN FRANCISCO

First published in the United States in 2012 by Chronicle Books LLC

Portions of this book were published in the United Kingdom in 2009 by Summersdale Publishers Ltd. under the title *Blackboard Blunders*. Copyright © 2009 by Summersdale Publishers Ltd. All rights reserved.

Compilation copyright © 2012 by Chronicle Books LLC.

Library of Congress Cataloging-in-Publication Data

Benson, Richard.
  F for effort! : more of the very best totally wrong test answers / Richard Benson.
    p. cm.
  ISBN 978-1-4521-1322-7
  1. Educational tests and measurements—Humor. 2. Questions and answers—Humor. I. Title.
LB3060.B46 2012
  371.26—dc23

                              2012010331

Manufactured in China

Cover design by Neil Egan
Book design by Liam Flanagan

FSC
MIX
Paper from
responsible sources
FSC® C008047
www.fsc.org

10 9 8

Chronicle Books LLC
680 Second Street
San Francisco, California 94107
www.chroniclebooks.com

CONTENTS

Introduction	7
Elementary Grades	9
High School	37
Biology	39
Chemistry	57
English	67
History and Geography	77
Math	97
Physics	109
Extra Credit	119

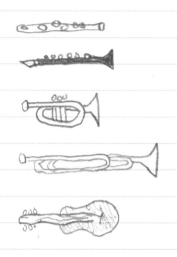

INTRODUCTION

There are different flavors of failure.

For the real test and homework responses collected here from the elementary school set, the failure is a lack of understanding why what they wrote is funny, as in the difference between "gravity" and "gravy." And in fact some of the mistakes yield deeper truths, such as the case of a student claiming J. K. Rowling is her "heroin."

The failures of the older students are merely that they have not successfully provided the correct answers to the questions they've been asked. Whatever. Instead, knowing as everyone does at some point that they just don't know the answer, they accomplish something perhaps more difficult, and certainly more fun. Thankfully, in mining the test prompts for humor, value, and artistic inspiration— math seems particularly stimulating in this regard— they've turned test taking and failing into a form of entertainment, for them, and now for us.

I  SCHOOL

The teacher likes to snivel around on a black chair in his office.

If you are really naughty you get exploded from school.

Once there was a dog in the playground and we went to smoke it but the lunch lady told us to keep away.

Today I painted an octopuss with big eyes and eight purple testicles.

You have to boo early for the school play.

There was a very thick frog on the
roads last night and it maid a
car crash into a bus.

there was an acident on our road
last night and a man was badly
enjoyed.

and at the end of the show
we all sing away in a manager.

I luv J. K. Rolling,
she is my heroin.

The pilot was bound to crash the
plane. The moment he saw his
wig come loose and fall to the
ground he knew there was no
chance of survival.

Two halves make a whale.

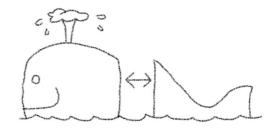

The north pole is so cold that the people that live there have to live sumewhere else.

You use the 24 hour clock in summer because it stays light longer.

In geography we learned that countries with sea round them are islands and ones without sea are incontinents.

They used to think the earth was fat but it is really round. It is shaped like a spear.

One of the most important farces is the farce that pulls things to the ground. This farce is called gravy

If there are alans out in space I would like for them to come to earth and say hello. Or whatever you say if you are an alan.

Sir Walter Raleigh circumcised the world with a big clipper.

The sun rises in the east and sets in the west. That is why it's hotter in the east.

Every morning dad has a slice of dread before he goes to work.

You can make toste by putting bread in a toster or by putting it under a girl until it is done.

SOMETIMES IN THE WAR THEY TAKE PRISNERS AND KEEP THEM AS OSTRIGES UNTIL THE WAR IS OVER.

The sultanas had wifes

and also porcupines

<u>Greek Gods</u>
The three gods in my project are the king of gods — Zeus, the messenger of the gods — Herpes, and the god of war — Mars.

We spend two weeks in grease every year.

My uncle is impotent.

He is the boss of a big factory.

My uncle shouts at my cussins and makes them do chors. One day they are going to be polisemen and polisewomen so they can put him in prison.

The most famus of the ten commendments is thou shall comment on a duckery.

I asked my mum why we said old men at the end of prayers at skool, I don't know any old men apart from grandpa.

Every living thing is an orgasm.
from the smallest cell to a
whole mammal, there are
orgasms everywhere.

I like to pick up smells on the
beach and keep them in my room.

The best place to put pants is somewhere warm and damp, where they can live happily.

The jungles of Africa are very dangerous for the people who explore them. There must be hundreds of people who have been mauled to death by a tiger or wino.

If you had no money in the 1930s you could get some by going to the porn shop. The man at the porn shop had 3 balls hanging over his entrance.

Then Joan of Ark met her end. She was burned as a steak.

I hepled my dad in garage. He let me hit some nails in with his hamster.

My mom falled down the stairs and was lyung prostitute on the ground.

and then Mr. Browning showed us how climbers use tampons to grip on to their rock.

My mom saw my messy bedroom and said it was abdominal. I felt a lot of quilt.

Dad was working in the garden and he ~~word~~ ascked mom if she could come and give him a hard.

My mom was a bit shook up yesterday because she had a dump in the car.

I have lots of fiends at school and I have even more fiends at home.

We are taking my little sister to see Satan this weekend.

Some of the biggest fish my dad had caught are from our holidays. He has caught pikes and craps.

Wen we were in Scotland we used to go into the woods for a walk. Dad liked to see how many beers he could see.

I wuld like to be a vet becouse I enjoy mrating animals.

My sister is a babyseller. She gets money from the grown ups, and sells their babys while they are away. I would like to be a baby-seller too.

WHEN I AM OLDER I WANT TO LEARN TO DRIVE A CAT.

I dident get to sleep mutch because next doors dog was baking all night.

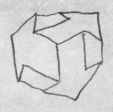

Subject: BIOLOGY

SCIENCE SUX

Can a man still reproduce with only one testicle?

No, girls don't find that attractive.

Name the largest bone in your body.

Franklin Witherston III

Name three uses of the skin.

Makes your appearence more
normal.

It doesn't show your
ribs or your insides.

It keeps part of the
wind from getting in

Name an insect.

a worm.

Name another insect.

another worm.

Name two kinds of ants.

Insects and Lady Uncles

Draw a plant cell and identify its most important parts.

The early sexual maturity of children and the subsequent shortening of childhood is caused by

Michael Jackson

Define post-mortem.

After twelve o'clock

What are steroids?

They keep your carpets still on the stairs.

Give the meaning of the term caesarean section.

its a distict in Rome

Name four animals that belong to the cat family.

The Momma Cat,
the poppa Cat,
and 2 Kittens

What is the general width of a hair follicle?

a hair's breadth.

What is ecology?

It's the bacteria in raw beef that makes you sick.

Cite the key difference between a centipede and a millipede.

Centipedes are found by the hundreds while millipedes are found by the millions.

What are fossils?

Fossils are extinct animals. The older it is, the more extinct it is!

What are crabs, lobsters, and crayfish all classified as?

They are all crushed asians.

Name four methods of locomotion in animals.

forwards
backwards
sideways
up and down

How frequent is biennial?

twice every so often

List five ways that plants interact with each other.

They don't. They're plants.
They can't talk or hang out.
Is this a trick question?

What is the science of classifying living things called?

RACISM.

What is a parabola?

A very horrible disease that monkeys carry.

What is your opinion of the relative merits of lecture and laboratory instruction in physiology?

My opinion of the relative merits of lecture and laboratory instruction in physiology is good.

Define germination.

to become a
German citizen.

In flowers, what function does the pistil serve?

It's a type of gun the flower
uses to defend itself against
bees

Give the precise location of cytochrome c in the cell.

After 3 blocks, take a left
at cytochrome b, then you'll see
cytochrome c down to your right.

Describe how an enzyme could be immobilized

Break its legs and tell
it to stay out of your
neighterhood.

Name one advantage that sexual reproduction has over asexual reproduction.

It feels good.

How is the brain like a cantaloupe?

It is DELICIOUS.

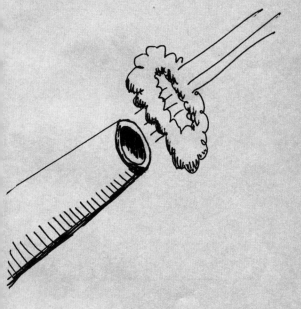

CHEMISTRY

Describe the bonding of SO_2.

It's pretty awesome.

Alice places a prepared slide on her microscope, but when she looks into it, she can't see anything. Suggest one reason why not.

She is blind.

How would you keep wine from turning into vinegar?

Drink it

Write a balanced equation for the reaction by writing balanced half equations and combining them.

$$MnO_4 \longrightarrow Something$$

$$Something\ else \longrightarrow Another\ thing$$

$$Stuff \longrightarrow other\ stuff$$

Explain how to measure less than 100 ml. of water using a graduated cylinder.

Carefully.

A liter is

a nest of puppies.

What is a super-saturated solution?

a solution that holds more than it can hold

Explain why phosphorus trichloride (PCl_3) is polar.

God made it that way.

When a child swallows a cleaning product, why is milk often given?

To make them happy before they die ☺

What is the toxicity of cyanide?

Cyanide is so poisonous that one drop of it on a dogs tongue will kill the strongest man.

What is the primary leavening agent used in bread?

AIR

What state of matter is steam?

Water gone crazy!

In which of the two steps does reduction of titanium occur?

2

Explain your answer.

The calcuable probability of getting this answer correct was 50%.

Dextromethorphan is also used and abused "recreationally" because, at larger doses, it is a hallucinogenic (it is structurally related to morphine). Due to a mistake in the weighing process, the solution the pharmacist has prepared is actually 0.0110 M in dextromethorphan. How will the pharmacist obtain 200 mL of safe children's syrup from the dangerous concentrated solution?

The pharmacist will

take the dangerous concentration and enjoy a free buzz!

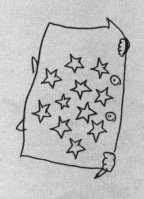

Subject: <u>ENGLISH</u> ....

Use the words timorous and meander in a sentence.

Timorous went to the Woods and Meander Went with him

Correct the error in the sentence: The girl were extraordinarily intelligent.

The boy were extremely intelligent.

Correct the following: The bull and the cow is in the field.

The cow and the
bull is in the field.
(Ladies come first.)

Give an example of the Imperative Mood.

Come up and see me
some time!

Why did the Ancient Mariner kill the albatross?

Nine days is a long time to have to clean bird poop off the deck.

Name two plays by Shakespeare.

Romeo and Juliet

Correct the sentence: The toast was drank in silence.

The toast was eat in silence.

Name three relative pronouns.

My aunt, my uncle, and my brother

Define caucus.

A dead animal.

Define monsoon.

a French gentleman

What is an inverted sentence?

One that makes sense either way.

Define epitaph.

A short sarcastic poem.

In what circumstances does the fourth act of *Hamlet* begin?

It starts immediately after the third act.

What is a morality play?

A play in which the characters are goblins, ghosts, virgins and other supernatural creatures.

What are Milton's significant works?

Milton wrote Paradise Lost.
Then his wife died
and he wrote Paradise
Regained.

Who was the Hunchback of Notre Dame?

One of the greatest football players

HISTORY AND GEOGRAPHY

Subject: ....

What people live in the Po Valley?

What did Paul Revere say at the end of his famous ride?

Whoa!

Explain one reason why people are concerned about rising water levels in the world's oceans.

Dolphins will invade coastal cities in phase 1 of their plan for world domination.

Explain why the population increased so much in nineteenth century Britain.

It was a very sexy time.

Describe a major social movement from the twentieth century and its effects.

The Great Bowel Movement of the 1950's left the populace feeling satisfied and lighter on the whole.

What hemisphere do you live in?

I don't live in a hemisphere, I live in an APARTMENT.

What is the chief product of the Hawaiian Islands?

rain fall.

Who signed the Magna Carta?

not me!

How many wars were waged against Spain?

6

Enumerate them.

1, 2, 3, 4, 5, 6

Cite three differences between the Arctic and Antarctic oceans.

The Antarctic Ocean has ants in it.

Name a check that is placed on the President's power in the United States.

If he doesn't do what the people want, his paycheck will bounce

What is the Sound west of the state of Washington?

the sound of the ocean.

What was the cause of the Industrial Revolution?

people stopped reproducing
by hand and started
reproducing by machines.

Name a right guaranteed under the Constitution.

the right to bare arms

What was the Age of Pericles?

I think he was about forty.

What made the tower of Pisa lean?

it skips lunch.

In what regions is Buddhism primarily practiced?

Budapest

The wife of a marquis is a

mayonnaise

What is meant by the legal term "Double Jeopardy"?

All the questions are North twice as much.

x 2

What two revolutions preceded the French Revolution?

The revolution of the Earth around the Sun and the revolution of the Moon around the Earth.

What law was common to all of the Colonies?

 gravitation

On what grounds was Aaron Burr tried for treason?

New York

What part did the U.S. Navy play in the war?

It played the star spangled banner.

What were Caesar's last words?

boo hoo, Brutus.

What direction does the Amazon flow?

Downhill. Rivers never flow uphill

What do the people of North Dakota raise?

Children.

When did the founding fathers draft the Constitution?

It was a second round pick, right after LeBron James.

Imagine that you lived at the same time as Abraham Lincoln. What would you say to him or ask him?

I'd tell him not to go to a play ever !

Name the system of writing used by ancient Egyptians.

Hydraulics.

What is the difference between the February and
October Revolutions?

The difference between
the Feb. Revolution and
the October revolution
is that one occurred in
Feb and one occurred
in October.

The government relocated the Indians to

reServoirs

What groups of people and which countries make up Scandinavia?

Scandinavia is made up of Danish people from Denmark, Norwegians from Norway, and Lapdancers from Lapland.

What are the Western plains noted for?

They are noted for their vast plains

Where is Chicago?

right now, they're in fifth place.

MATH

Subject: ....

The solid figure below can best be described as:

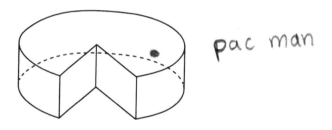

pac man

Anna is trying to decide what to have for lunch in the cafeteria. She can choose 1 entrée and 2 side dishes. There are 4 available entrées, and 8 available side dishes. How many different combinations are possible for Anna's lunch?

None. She has savere food allegies and can only eat oatmeal.

A polygon is:

A Man who has many wifes

John keeps pigs and chickens on his farm. Among them, they have a total of 43 heads and 142 legs. How many pigs and chickens are on the farm?

Two total: one pig with 41 heads and 5 legs, and one chicken with 2 heads and 137 legs.

If an angle has less than 90 degrees, what is it called?

A cute angle.

Name a pair of vertical angles.

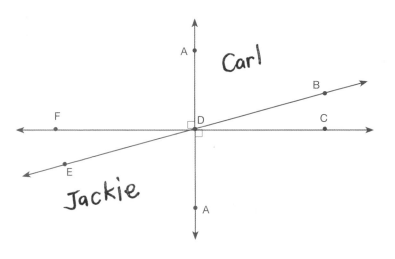

A startled armadillo jumps straight into the air with an initial velocity of 18 feet per second. After how many seconds does it land on the ground?

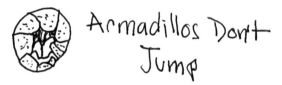 Armadillos Don't Jump

What do we mean by "total" and "remainder"?

THE TOTAL IS WHEN YOU ADD UP ALL THE NUMBERS AND THE REMAINDER IS AN ANIMAL THAT PULLS SANTA'S SLEIGH.

A train is blowing its whistle while traveling at 33 m/s. The speed of sound is 343 m/s. If you are directly in front of the train, what is the whistle frequency you hear?

you will get hit by the train before you can even figure out what that whistling sound is.

Matt had a 9 ft by 12 ft wall painted. For a wall twice as wide, the painter charged him twice as much. Is this reasonable? Explain.

The painter can charge whatever he wants. If Matt doesn't like it, he can paint his own walls.

What is the unique solution to the IVP $\begin{cases} y(0) = 19 \\ y' = 0.85y \end{cases}$?

it is secret.

Find the complex and real roots of the function:
$f(x) = x^2 (x^3 - 1)$

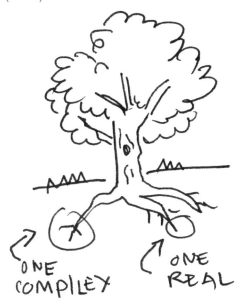

ONE COMPLEX

ONE REAL

Find the volume and surface area of the right cylinder.

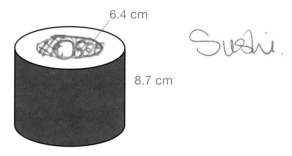

6.4 cm

8.7 cm

Sushi.

If Andrew invests $25,000 at 8.5% APR compounded monthly, how much money will he have after 10 years?

$0, with the economy like it is.

Define the triangle.

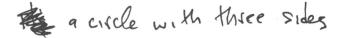 a circle with three sides

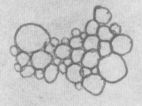

Define electronegativity.

The vibe robots give off when they're in a bad mood.

What causes earthquakes?

Fat kids chasing the ice cream truck.

The water of the earth's oceans stores lots of heat. An engineer designed an ocean liner that would extract heat from the ocean's waters at Th = 10oC (283 K) and reject heat to the atmosphere at T1 = 20oC (293 K). He thought he had a good idea, but his boss fired him. Explain.

Because he slept with his boss' wife.

Describe an achievement of Galileo.

He invented the
solar system.

What is a solar day?

SUNday

Why are there rings around Saturn?

God liked it,
so he put a ring on it.

Name three sources of heat.

FIRE

FRICTION

HELL

Explain the effect of heat and cold and give an illustration.

Heat expands — the days are longer in the summer

cold contrats - the days are shorter in winter!

Explain how energy is lost during an energy conversion.

Thinking about an energy conversion is so boring that I completely run out of energy and have to go to sleep at my desk.

Define momentum.

Something that you give someone when they are going away

Name three states in which water may exist.

New York
New Jersey
Pennsylvania

What causes thunder?

Clouds burping

BURP

How are clouds formed?

I AM NOT SURE HOW CLOUDS
GET FORMED BUT THE CLOUDS
KNOW HOW TO DO IT, AND THAT
'S THE IMPORTANT THING

What are the tides?

the tides are a fight between
the Earth and the moon. All water
tends towards the moon, because
there is no water in the moon,
and nature abhors a vacuum.
I forget where the sun joins
in this fight.

EXTRA CREDIT

Subject: ....

Explain this sentence: Be kind to the erring.

"The erring" means "the Irish"
so the sentence means:
Be kind to the Irish.

What is the chief cause of divorce?

Marriage

Science Question:

Why does CO_2 put out fire?

Brief description of your experiment plan/research plan:

CO_2 puts out fire.

Any safety issues or unique display requirements? (If so, describe below.)

There is going to be a fire!

How are sardines caught?

you just throw the
little cans overboard

Why is the sea salty?

Because it has so many
fish in it.

Fossil fuels are usually associated with which of the three major rock types?

DINOSAURS.

When a star in the sky suddenly brightens and then fades gradually over several years, what is likely happening in the star's life cycle?

It's probably having a hot flash and is going through menopause.

Name three articles of clothing.

A shirt and a pair of pants.

CAUSE:
Tony practices the piano 20 minutes every day.

EFFECT:

He is a BIG NERD.

An alien becomes a citizen by the process of

Ferthlizthon

What should be done in a case of apparent drowning?

Take the parent out of the water.

In the space below please write any overall comments about this course or instructor not covered above.

If I had one hour to live, I'd spend it in this class because it feels like an eternity.

the panda will
cry if I get a
bad grade.
Boo-hoo

Cheer him up by
studying for the
final.

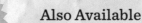

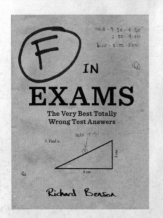